Little Sister, Big Mess!

Written by Jane E. Gerver
Illustrated by Shelley Dieterichs

Children's Press®
A Division of Scholastic Inc.
New York • Toronto • London • Auckland • Sydney
Mexico City • New Delhi • Hong Kong
Danbury, Connecticut

To Nina, who likes baking cookies—both thick and thin.
—J. E. G.

To all my good buddies
—S. D.

Reading Consultant

Cecilia Minden-Cupp, PhD
Former Director of the Language and Literacy Program
Harvard Graduate School of Education
Cambridge, Massachusetts

Cover design: The Design Lab
Interior design: Herman Adler

Library of Congress Cataloging-in-Publication Data

Gerver, Jane E.
  Little sister, big mess! / by Jane E. Gerver; illustrated by Shelley
Dieterichs ; reading consultant, Cecilia Minden-Cupp.
     p. cm. — (A rookie reader: opposites)
  ISBN-13: 978-0-531-17545-3 (lib. bdg.)   978-0-531-17779-2 (pbk.)
  ISBN-10: 0-531-17545-6 (lib. bdg.)   0-531-17779-3 (pbk.)
  1. English language—Synonyms and antonyms—Juvenile literature.
I. Dieterichs, Shelley. II. Title. III. Series.
  PE1591.G42 2007
  423'.12—dc22   2006025602

CHILDREN'S PRESS, and A ROOKIE READER®, and associated logos
are trademarks and/or registered trademarks of Scholastic Library
Publishing. SCHOLASTIC and associated logos are trademarks and/or
registered trademarks of Scholastic Inc.
1 2 3 4 5 6 7 8 9 10 R 16 15 14 13 12 11 10 09 08 07

I am a big brother.
I am tall.

This is my little sister.
She is short.

We like to bake cookies.

8

I take down a bowl.
She picks up a spoon.

The butter is hard!
Mash, mash.
Now the butter is soft.

We add light brown sugar.
Then we add dark brown sugar.
Mix, mix.

She adds wet eggs.
I add dry flour.
Stir, stir!

We add chocolate chips.
Yum, yum!

She takes a tray from the low shelf.
I take a tray from the high shelf.

We drop batter on the trays.
I make thin drops.
My sister makes thick drops.

We put the trays in the oven.
I use a black mitt.
My sister uses a white mitt.

Are the cookies ready?
No, they're not ready yet.

We take the trays out.

One tray cools here.
The other cools there.

Cold milk . . .
warm cookies . . .
little sister . . .
big mess!

Word List (85 words)

(Words in **bold** are used as opposites.)

a	cools	**little**	oven	**there**
add	**dark**	**low**	picks	they're
adds	**down**	make	put	**thick**
am	drop	makes	ready	**thin**
are	drops	mash	she	this
bake	**dry**	mess	shelf	to
batter	eggs	milk	**short**	tray
big	flour	mitt	**sister**	trays
black	from	mix	**soft**	**up**
bowl	**hard**	my	spoon	use
brother	**here**	no	stir	uses
brown	**high**	not	sugar	**warm**
butter	I	now	take	we
chips	**in**	on	takes	**wet**
chocolate	is	one	**tall**	white
cold	**light**	other	the	yet
cookies	like	**out**	then	yum

About the Author

Jane E. Gerver is the author of many children's books, ranging from preschool board books to middle-grade fiction. She lives with her husband and little daughter in New York City.

About the Illustrator

Whimsical, lovable pets, and children are the hallmarks of Shelley's children's illustrations. Shelley resides in Saint Louis, Missouri, with her husband and cats Fred and Ethel. She also loves chocolate chip cookies.